CONTENTS

CHAPTER 1
ACTION!

Action movies are exciting to watch! An action hero leaps from a burning building. A car flies through the air and smashes into a truck!

It looks as if the actors do these stunts. In fact, most stunts are performed by stuntmen and women.

Stunt performers take the place of actors. They perform stunts that are too difficult or too dangerous for the actors to do.

Stuntman Greg Brazzell drives a car into a truck filled with water bottles.

CHAPTER 2

MOVIE STUNTS TIMELINE

1900s TO 1930s

At first, Hollywood actors performed their own stunts in their movies. Audiences loved these action scenes. So, film directors began to use stunt performers.

Rose Wenger was a rodeo rider. She doubled for an actress called Helen Holmes in a Western movie serial.

Rose Wenger

1940s TO 1950s

Film directors wanted more amazing stunts.

Performers developed ways to make stunts as safe as possible.

They used trampolines, cardboard boxes and straw to break high falls.

1960s to 1970s

New technology was developed to make stunts look more real. Air rams and air bags were invented.

Air rams throw a performer into the air.

Air ram

1980s to 1990s

Action films, such as *Rambo, Indiana Jones* and *Die Hard*, became very popular. They were packed with stunts and special effects.

A member of a stunt crew tests a flying vest

Many films used wire work stunts.
The performers fly through the air on wires.

 If you do CGI and real stunt work together, you can do fantastic things.

Joel Silver, Hollywood Producer

2000s

Many film directors now use computers to make realistic action scenes. But real stunts are still popular!

The Matrix movies mix computer generated imagery (CGI), wire work and martial arts.

Wires

Green screen

The actors were filmed against a green screen.
Then a background was added using a computer.
The wires were removed by computer, too.
The actors look as if they are flying above the ground.

CHAPTER 3

STUNT STARS

Buster Keaton
Lived 1895 to 1966

Buster Keaton was a silent film actor. He did many of his own stunts. In this famous scene, a house falls on Keaton. The house misses Keaton because he is standing below an open window.

Yakima Canutt
Lived 1895 to 1986

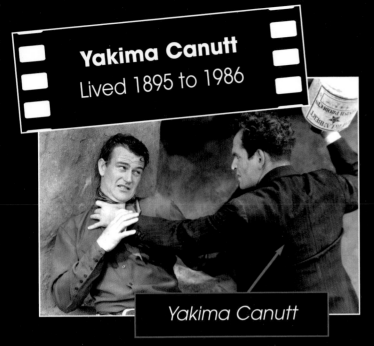

Yakima Canutt

Canutt did his first film stunt in 1915. He got his last film credit in 1975! Canutt and his friend the actor John Wayne developed fighting and stunt techniques.

Pearl White
Lived 1889 to 1938

Pearl White was an actress who did many of her own stunts. She starred in *The Perils of Pauline*.

Her most famous stunt was when she was tied to railroad tracks in front of a speeding train!

Dar Robinson
Lived 1947 to 1986

Robinson does tricks on a trampoline hanging from a helicopter

In 1980, Dar Robinson jumped off the CN Tower in Toronto, Canada. He did this stunt for the movie *High Point*. His hidden parachute opened just 90 metres from the ground!

Dar Robinson liked to set stunt records. He was the first person to sky dive out of a plane at 3,600 metres while riding in a small sports car.

CN Tower

Jackie Chan
Born in 1954

Jackie Chan started his career as a stuntman in Bruce Lee Kung Fu movies.

Chan's movies mix slapstick comedy with Kung Fu action.

CHAPTER 4

A CAREER IN STUNTWORK

This is Steve Truglia. He is a stunt performer and stunt co-ordinator. Stunt co-ordinators plan the stunts for action scenes in movies and TV shows.

> " Today I'm planning a fight scene for a new movie. The stunt must look real but it must also be as safe as possible. "
> *Steve Truglia*

PLANNING A STUNT

- I read the script and make notes on the action scenes.

- I discuss how the stunt should look with the film director.

- I work out how much the stunt will cost.

- I visit the film location. This is called a "recce".

- I choose the stunt performers.

On the day of a shoot, the stunt performers practise the stunt.

In a stunt fight, the performer's hand never makes contact with the face.

Skilled stunt performers and clever camera angles make a stunt fight look real.

A good stunt is based on strong team work. Often, on big movies, a separate film crew works on the action scenes. This is called the "Second Unit".

" When I'm planning a stunt, safety is everything. I have to think what if... **"**

Steve Truglia

In the fight scene, one of the stunt performers will be thrown through a window.

Film sets have windows and items such as bottles made from special materials. These materials smash easily and safely. They are known as "breakaway effects".

This is rubber glass. It can be torn or crumbled into pieces.

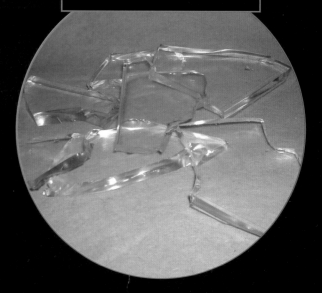

A stuntman crashes through breakaway glass.

" People who take risks don't make good stunt performers.

I'm a very careful person. I make sure that my stunts are set up as safely as possible. I practise my stunts before I perform them.

The last few minutes before I perform a stunt are tense. There is a lot of pressure.

You have to do it – and you have to do it right. There might be 150 people watching you! "

Steve Truglia

Steve Truglia gets ready to do a driving stunt.

Stuntmen and women learn to drive at high speeds. They learn how to skid, spin and even drive on two wheels!

" When you perform a stunt, you must focus on the stunt. Nothing matters but what you're doing! "

Steve Truglia

This car "knock-down" stunt is dangerous. Steve plans every second and practises every move he makes.

STUNTS AND SAFETY

Many movies have scenes where people are on fire. These are called burn scenes. They are very dangerous to perform.

The stunt performers wear fireproof clothes. They use a special gel to stop their skin and hair burning.

The performers must not breathe when they are on fire. They could burn their lungs or breathe in poisonous fumes.

The burn is carefully timed. People trained to give medical help stand by, in case of an emergency. The stunt crew is ready to put out the fire.

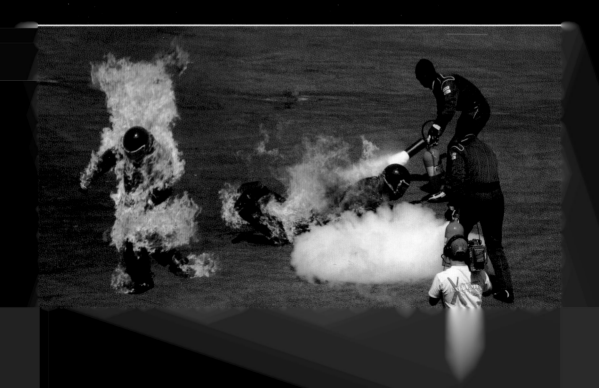

Stuntman Steve Truglia performs a fire burn

High fall stunts are very dangerous. Every second of the fall is planned, practised and tested.

Stunt performers learn how to fall and how to land.

If a stunt performer lands in the wrong position, they can be badly hurt.

Air bag

Giant air bags give stunt performers a safe place to land during "high fall" stunts.

A "safety spotter" keeps watch from out of view of the camera. Safety spotters are normally other stunt performers.

If a stunt performer gets into trouble, the spotter is ready to help.

A safe landing

The person jumping knows that everything is safe. However, they still need the courage to jump!

CHAPTER 6

SUPER STUNTS

Stunt performers are always pushing themselves to the limit.

The 1959 movie *Ben Hur* features a Roman chariot race.
Yakima Canutt directed the race.
His son Joe was one of the stunt performers.

The chariot race in Ben Hur

During the race, Joe Canutt's chariot was bumped by another chariot. He nearly fell out. Canutt could have been crushed by the racing chariots.

The bump was planned, but Canutt's near fatal fall wasn't!

Bud Ekins was Steve McQueen's double
for this scene from *The Great Escape*.

Ekins had to jump a motorbike
over a barbed wire fence.

Sébastien Foucan is a parkour expert.
Parkour involves running, jumping and climbing
over obstacles such as buildings.

Sébastien Foucan

Foucan starred in the opening chase scene
from the James Bond movie, *Casino Royale*.

CHAPTER 7
STUNT DOUBLES

Stunt co-ordinators choose stunt performers for two important reasons:

- **They are trained and insured to do the stunt.**
- **They are a good "double" for the actor.**

Debbie Evans is a top Hollywood stuntwoman.
She is also a champion motorbike rider.

Carrie-Anne
Moss

Debbie Evans was the stunt double for actress
Carrie-Anne Moss in The Matrix Reloaded.

Most stunt performers get paid by the day or by the week. Some performers get contracts for longer periods of time.

Sophia Crawford got a contract for a complete TV series. She was the stunt double for Sarah Michelle Gellar in 78 episodes of *Buffy the Vampire Slayer*.

Sophia Crawford practises Buffy's moves

Sarah Michelle Gellar

CHAPTER 8
007 STUNTS

Not all actors need a stunt double all of the time! Daniel Craig is the latest actor to play James Bond.

In *Casino Royale* and *Quantum of Solace*, Craig wanted to perform as many of his own stunts as possible.

In *Casino Royale* the stunts included a stair fall and an underwater rescue scene. Craig got bruises and cuts and even lost a tooth.

" If you don't get bruised playing Bond, you're not doing it properly. **"**

Daniel Craig

Wires

Padding

Craig leaps from a rooftop
in Quantum of Solace

NEED TO KNOW WORDS

air bag A giant bag filled with air. It provides a safe place to land.

air ram A piece of equipment that throws a performer into the air.

Bruce Lee A martial arts expert who made martial arts popular in movies.

camera angle The position from which the camera shoots the film.

computer generated imagery (CGI)
Realistic-looking images that have been created using a computer.

contract An agreement, in law, between people.

credit A film credit is when a person's name is shown at the end of a film.

director The person who chooses the actors and tells them what to do in each scene of a movie, play or TV show. The director also decides how the cameras should film the scenes.

double Someone who takes an actor's place in a movie.

insured If you are insured it means you have paid money into a fund in case something bad happens to you.
If something bad does happen, the fund pays money to help you.

location The place where a movie or TV show is filmed.

martial arts Ways of fighting without weapons, such as Kung Fu, karate and judo.

rodeo A contest in which cowboys show off their horse riding skills.

script The words the actors say in a movie, play or TV show.

slapstick Comedy based on people being clumsy on purpose – for example, falling over or bumping into things.

special effects Tricks that movie-makers use to make the audience think that something is real in a movie.

technique A way of doing something.